MW01629235

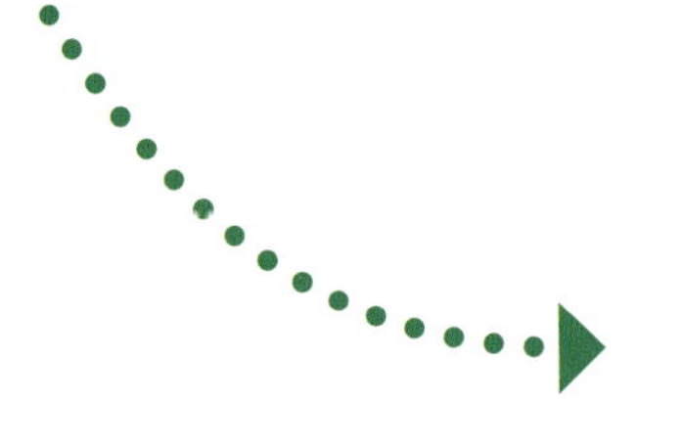

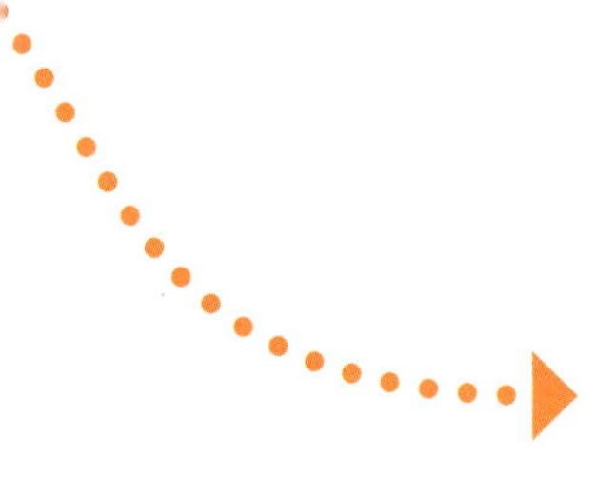

Your Job at School

You have an important job, too! Your job is to learn as much as you can. You can help yourself learn.

What if this were your class? What would you do so you could learn?

What if this were your class? What would you do so you could learn?

Work carefully.

Think about what you're doing.

Do your best.

Pay attention to your teacher.

Listen to others.

Community Workers

Workers in the community do many jobs.
See if you can match the worker with the job.

I'm a firefighter. Can you guess my job?

I'm a police officer. Can you guess my job?

I'm a bus driver. Can you guess my job?

I'm a mail carrier. Can you guess my job?

I deliver letters and small packages to people.
MAPLE ST.
I drive a bus and take people places.
I put out fires.
I make the community safe.

More Community Workers

Look at all the workers. They're on their way to work right now.

This is Dr. Ramos. She helps sick people.

This is nurse Jason Ling. He helps the doctors take care of sick people.

This is Eve Angler. She's a carpenter. She builds and fixes things made from wood.

This is Cory Crew. He's a mechanic. He fixes people's cars.

This is Dana McDivett. She works in a store.

Where is each person going?

Worker Animals

Animals can work, too. A dog can guide a person on the street. A monkey can help someone with medicine. A therapy dog can give love to people in hospitals.

Workers Solve Problems

Want to play a game? This game is about community workers who solve problems.

How to Play

- Close your eyes and put your finger on a number.
- Move that number of spaces on the game board.
- Look at the picture where you land. Tell about the problem.
- Name the community worker who can solve the problem.

Jobs Today and Long Ago

Some jobs are the same today as they were long ago. Some jobs are different.

Long ago, cobblers made shoes by hand.

Today, workers use machines to make shoes. People buy the shoes at a shoe store.

A miller was someone who ground wheat into flour. Long ago, people brought wheat to the miller.

Today, workers use machines to grind wheat into flour. People buy flour at the store.

Some jobs are not needed anymore.

Long ago, lamplighters would light streetlights. Today, streetlights are electric, and do not need people to light them.

Long ago, people would tap on a window to wake up the person living there. Today, we have alarm clocks.

Long ago, log drivers helped move logs downriver. Today, we use trains and trucks.

Why People Work

People get money for the work they do. People use money to pay for goods and services.

The bricklayer works.

She earns money for the work she does.

The florist works.

The florist earns money for his work.

She chooses things to buy.

She uses money she earned to pay for the things.

The florist wants to get his hair cut.

He uses money he earned to pay for the haircut.

Activities

TO THE TEACHER

INTERVIEW

Ask children to describe the jobs of adult family members or other adults they know, such as neighbors. Ask: What questions would you ask if you wanted to find out more about the person's job? Write the questions on the board. Suggest that children use the questions to interview a family member or neighbor about their job. Afterward, allow time for children to share what they learned about the jobs during a class career day.

WHEN I GROW UP

Invite children to think about the kind of work they would like to do when they grow up. Talk about where the work is done, what the worker wears, the tools the worker may use, and why the work is important. Have children use their ideas to illustrate a book entitled, *When I Grow Up*. Encourage children to present their finished books to classmates and share their ideas.

MAKE CONNECTIONS WITH THESE RELATED TITLES

Being a Good Citizen

Working together. Doing your part. Showing respect. These are things that you do to be a good citizen in your neighborhood.

Neighborhoods

Fire stations. Schools. Supermarkets. Home. Together, these places make up a neighborhood. What is your neighborhood like?

Maps

You know your classroom. Right? What would a map of your classroom look like? You can find out right here!

LEARN MORE ONLINE!

- Crossing guards and custodians play an important role at school. What are their jobs?
- How do you use what you learn in school? Read online to find out!
- Play a game that matches community workers with the work they do.
- Long ago, the job of a shepherd was to watch and care for herds of animals. Read a story about a shepherd.

Houghton Mifflin Harcourt

hmhco.com

Editor: Jennifer Dixon
Art Direction: Brobel Design
Designers: Ian Brown, Ed Gabel, David Ricculli, Jeremy Rech
Photo Research: Ted Levine, Elisabeth Morgan
Activities Writer: Marjorie Frank
Proofreader: Jennifer Dixon
Fact-Checker: Marjorie Frank

Author: Marjorie Frank

President and CEO: Ted Levine
Chairman and Founder: Mark Levine

KINDERGARTEN TITLES

Being a Good Citizen

Flags and Other Symbols

Jobs

Maps

Neighborhoods

Past and Present

History: A Celebration

On the Cover: A delivery man prepares to deliver a hand truck full of boxes. **Shutterstock:** Mark LaMoyne.

Picture Credits: Alamy: Kumar Sriskandan: p.14 bottom right (buying flour); Chronicle: p.15 top left (lamplighter, 1808). **Getty Images:** Jim Craigmyle: p.10 (guide dog); Bettmann: p.11 top (monkey helping paralyzed man). **iStock:** monkeybusinessimages: p.2 top (teacher), p.3 bottom (cafeteria); DGLimages: p.3 (classroom); asiseeit: p.2 (principal); andresrimaging: p.2 bottom (librarian); FangXiaNuo: p.3 (library); jwblinn: p.3 top (office); kali9: p.6 upper left (firefighter); Montes-Bradley: p.6 upper right (police offficer); kali9: p.6 bottom left (bus driver); Yuri_Arcurs: p.6 bottom right (mail carrier); ilbusca: p.15 top right (street sweeper, Paris). **Library of Congress:** Van Norman, George H., photographer: p.14 upper left (Massachusetts cobbler). **National Scenic Byways Program:** Red Rouse: p.15 bottom (river drivers). **North Wind Picture Archives:** p.14 bottom left (old mill in Nantucket, 1800s). **Shutterstock:** Monkey Business Images: p.2 (cafeteria worker), p.4 (paying attention), p.5 (completing worksheets), p.11 bottom (therapy dog); risteski goce: p.14 top right (looking at shoes); Rvector: p.18 bottom (book icon); Diego Cervo: p.19 top left (group of friends); George W. Bailey: p.19 top center (fire engine and station); olenadesign: p.19 top right (city map); graphic-line: p.19 bottom (traffic guard).

Original Illustrations:
Michael Kline Illustration: Community Workers, p.7; More Community Workers, pp.8–9; Workers Solve Problems, pp.12–13; Why People Work, pp.16–17; Interview, p.18.

Printed in the U.S.A.

ISBN 978-1-328-81780-8

11 12 13 14 15 16 0029 27 26 25 24 23 22 21 20

4500797415 B C D E F G

ISBN 978-1-328-81780-8